The M.O.U.T.H. Book

Messages of Uplift to Heal

Quindell Evans

Copyright © 2018 by Quindell Evans

All rights reserved.

ISBN 978-1-387-52460-0

DR. BAP
(Don't Read…Before Asking Permission)

Respect the privacy of who owns this book. We learn to be open & honest with others through being open & honest with ourselves. This is a book where the owner freely expresses him or herself and reflects on him or herself for his or her own freedom and personal growth. **<u>The content of this book may be entirely private resulting in the owner feeling completely exposed no matter if you are a close friend or family member.</u>** If you weren't granted permission to read further by the owner of this book please don't go any further before asking. Thank you.

ACKNOWLEDGMENTS

M.O.U.T.H. stands for Messages of Uplift to Heal and began as a way for me to uplift myself using my poetic rhetoric. I like to sing and record music so all of the messages rhyme and have a rhythmic feel. I began to share them through text message with my immediate friends and acquaintances that showed much appreciation of my original quotes.

Kevin Perry, my Phi Beta Sigma Fraternity, Inc. brother thought of the idea to have weekly meetings where we can discuss art and business projects, which has grounded me tremendously. His charismatic attitude and unconditional support gave me the capacity to share these messages beyond my immediate friends.

Ann Christine Espino, my girlfriend, pushed me to be more spontaneous with my work and after teaching me basic yoga, it was in her living space where I began to actually record and make a list of the mantras I had created with the idea to write a book.

Malcolm Weaver, my cousin, always supported everything I have ever pursued since we were young children. His presence is enough to allow me to focus on my goals.

Joyce Evans, my mother, has always been a nurturer and is known to many as Mama Joyce or grandma for her willingness to be the village that raises a child. She inspires me by being her.

Curtis Harris, Danny King, Sharon Kennedy, Lisa Kenner & James Gansrow are mentoring adults who've always gave me a chance and provided me with love, support and opportunities.

Much love to my family who always supported my talent, my friends who show up to support me at shows, Preston and Priscilla who grounded me in my healing and everyone who ever gave a penny to me while I busked on the NYC trains.

1. I STAND GROUNDED AND READY TO RECEIVE ALL LOVE, LIGHT, HARMONY & HEALING THAT IS DUE UNTO ME.

WRITE DOWN A LIST OF GOALS YOU WANT TO COMPLETE. BE AS SPECIFIC AS YOU LIKE.

2. ANY PAIN THAT I FEEL OR SEE, LET IT BE TRANSFORMED AND TRANSCENDED INTO POSITIVITY.

MAKE A LIST OF THINGS YOU ABSOLUTELY DO NOT LIKE THEN SAY OUT LOUD THAT YOU LOVE THEM. IT'S CALLED SARCASM.
(Ex: I love when I miss the bus by a few seconds and have to wait for the next one.)

3. AS I MAKE A LIVING FOR ME, I ONLY ACCEPT AND RECEIVE LOVE, LIGHT AND POSITIVITY.

Quindell Evans

WHAT IS ONE PROBLEM IN THE WORLD AND WHAT IS ONE SOLUTION FOR IT?
(Ex: Problem: homelessness. Solution: affordable housing for everyone.)

4. THE DIFFERENCES OF OTHERS DOES NOT MAKE US SEPARATE. BECAUSE I ACCEPT IT, IT BRINGS US TOGETHER AND CONNECTS US.

DO YOU HAVE A PET? WHAT DO YOU LEARN FROM IT, THAT YOU CANT LEARN FROM A PERSON, BY OWNING ONE? WHAT DOES THE PET LEARN FROM YOU?

5. WHEN THE UNIVERSE CAUSES CHANGES AND I NEED HELP, I WILL SEEK THE KNOWLEDGE OF SELF.

MEDITATE: INHALE THROUGH YOUR NOSE FOR 7 SECONDS, HOLD YOUR BREATH FOR 5 SECONDS THEN EXHALE THROUGH YOUR MOUTH FOR 10 SECONDS. REPEAT THIS SEQUENCE, SITTING STILL WITH YOUR EYES CLOSED, UNTIL YOU FEEL IN CONTROL OF YOUR THOUGHTS.

6. WHEN YOU DON'T KNOW WHERE TO GO, BE STILL. BE UNMOVING. MOVE SLOW.

MEDITATE: INHALE THROUGH YOUR LEFT NOSTRIL FOR 7 SECONDS, WHILE HOLDING THE RIGHT NOSTRIL CLOSE…THEN HOLD BOTH FOR 3 SECONDS…THEN EXHALE THROUGH THE RIGHT NOSTRIL FOR 7 SECONDS. DO THE SAME STARTING WITH THE RIGHT NOSTRIL AND ENDING WITH THE LEFT NOSTRIL. REPEAT THIS SEQUENCE, SITTING STILL WITH YOUR EYES CLOSED, UNTIL YOU FEEL IN CONTROL OF YOUR THOUGHTS.

7. I HAVE RESPECT FOR OTHERS' PERSPECTIVES. I KNOW WHEN TO REVEAL MINE OR PROTECT IT.

DO YOU HAVE A ROOMMATE? WHAT IS YOUR RELATIONSHIP LIKE? WHAT SIMILARITIES AND DIFFERENCES DO YOU HAVE?

8. MY HARMONY WITH COMMUNICATION IN RELATIONSHIPS DEPENDS ON MY BALANCE AND SELF-CONTROL INNATELY.

WHAT'S YOUR FAVORITE EXERCISE? HOW OFTEN DO YOU EXERCISE? DO YOU THINK EXERCISING IS IMPORTANT?

9. AS I BALANCE AND HEIGHTEN MY VIBRATIONS, MAY THE UNIVERSE PROTECT ME FROM ANYTHING OR ANYONE THAT WANTS TO TAKE THEM.

DO YOU AGREE WITH OFFERING MONEY, FOOD OR HELP TO THE HOMELESS ON THE STREET? WHY?

10. IN ORDER TO HELP SOMEONE ELSE, IT BEGINS WITH HELPING MYSELF.

Quindell Evans

DO YOU DONATE TO ANY CHARITY? WHY OR WHY NOT?

11. I DON'T LOOK BACK ON MISTAKES WITH REGRET OR SORROW. I LOOK FORWARD WITH PASSION TO LIVING DIFFERENT TOMORROW.

IF YOU COULD TIME TRAVEL AND GIVE YOURSELF, FROM 5 YEARS AGO, ANY ADVICE, WHAT WOULD YOU SAY?

12. WHEN I PROVIDE SUPPORT FOR SOMEONE ALONG HIS OR HER PATH, THIS ALLOWS THE UNIVERSE TO GUIDE ME ALONG MY PATH.

ASK 5 PEOPLE, WHETHER FRIENDS, FAMILY OR STRANGERS WHAT THEY WANTED TO BE WHEN THEY WERE CHILDREN?

13. MAY ANY LEACHING, NEGATIVE OR DRAINING ENERGY OFF THE STREETS BE TRANSFORMED INTO POSITIVE ENERGY AND RELEASED.

MAKE A LIST OF THINGS YOU ABSOLUTELY DO NOT LIKE THEN SAY OUT LOUD THAT YOU LOVE THEM. IT'S CALLED SARCASM.
(Ex: I love when I miss the bus by a few seconds and have to wait for the next one.)

14. I FREE MYSELF OF ALL NEGATIVE HABITS AND MATERIAL ATTATCHMENTS BY LETTING GO AND TAKING CONTROL OF MY ACTIONS.

MAKE ONE LIST OF THINGS YOU LIKE TO DO, ANOTHER LIST OF YOUR FAVORITE THINGS TO EAT AND ONE MORE LIST OF YOUR MOST VALUABLE ITEMS OR POSSESSIONS. WHAT CAN YOU SEE YOURSELF WITHOUT?
(Ex: Watching TV, Cereal & Milk, and Car.)

15. WHEN WORKING WITH OTHERS TOWARD A GOAL, I ALLOW OUR DIFFERENCES TO BE COMPLIMENTARY TO THE WHOLE.

… Quindell Evans

WHAT ROLES DO YOU LIKE TO VOLUNTEER IN GROUP SETTINGS AND ACTIVITIES?

16. WHEN I FALL, I GET BACK UP AND KEEP RUNNING. FAILURE IS ONLY A TEST TO SEE HOW MUCH I WANT IT.

WHAT IS ONE THING YOU HAD TO TRY MORE THAN ONCE TO ACHIEVE AT?

17. I AM FULLY IN CONTROL OF THE WAY I AM LIVING. I AM THE MASTER OF MY CHOICES AND DECIONS.

Quindell Evans

DO YOU EVER FEEL LIKE YOU HAVE BAD LUCK? DO YOU EVER FEEL LIKE YOU HAVE GOOD LUCK?

18. TO REMAIN GROUNDED IN REALITY, I PREPARE BY MAKING PLANS. FOR THE THINGS I CAN'T DO ALONE, I ACCEPT A HELPING HAND.

Quindell Evans

IF YOU COULD ASK ONE PERSON FOR ADVICE, WHO WOULD IT BE?

19. WHEN I GO INSIDE OF MYSELF INSTEAD OF FOCUSING ON THE THINGS AROUND ME, I FIND OUT THE MOST AMAZING THINGS ABOUT ME.

WHAT ARE 5 (OR MORE) THINGS YOU'RE REALLY GOOD AT?

20. I BALANCE MY EMOTIONS SO I WONT FEAR IT IN ORDER TO FOCUS AND SEE MORE CLEARLY.

Quindell Evans

WHAT IS ONE REASON TO BE HAPPY INSTEAD OF SAD?

21. I MAKE PLANS TO MAKE IT TO WHERE I WANT TO BE. EVEN WHEN LIFE ISN'T, I STRIVE TO BE AS FAIR AS I CAN BE.

Quindell Evans

WHERE DO YOU SEE YOURSELF IN 5 YEARS? HOW DO YOU PLAN ON GETTING THERE?

22. I WALK WITH THE CONFIDENCE OF THE SUN. I WILL RISE TO MY GOALS EVERYDAY AND SHINE UNTIL IT'S DONE.

WHAT IS SOMETHING YOU'VE ALWAYS WANTED TO DO BUT YOU HAVE NO CLUE ON WHERE TO START? DESCRIBE 3 REASONS WHY YOU WANT TO DO IT.

23. I HAVE INNER PEACE AND PATIENCE BECAUSE I MOVE WITH A PURPOSEFUL PLAN ALONG A PATH WITH PEOPLE I TRUST TO PROVIDE A HELPING HAND.

Quindell Evans

WHAT'S THE DIFFERENCE BETWEEN A FRIEND AND A PEER?

24. PRACTICAL HABITS WITH REFLECTION TENDS TO MAKE PERFECTION. I PRACTICE FLOWING WITH THE WIND TO MASTER MY DIRECTION.

WHAT IS SOMETHING THAT YOU FEEL YOU'RE NATURALLY GOOD AT? WHAT IS SOMETHING YOU HAD TO PRACTICE TO BECOME GOOD AT?

**25. I AM FILLED WITH LOVE INSIDE OF ME BUT THE OUTSIDE IS WHAT YOU SEE.
I LOOK A DIRTY FILTHY SWAMP AND SEE ITS LIFE-GIVING BEAUTY.**

Quindell Evans

WHAT'S ONE FOOD, DRINK OR DESSERT THAT LOOKED NASTY UNTIL YOU TASTED IT?

26. I DON'T GAMBLE WITH MY LIFE AND PLAY WITH IT. I INVEST IN MYSELF AND TAKE RISKS.

WHAT ARE SOME THINGS YOU WANT TO STOP DOING? WHAT ARE SOME THINGS YOU WANT TO CONTINUE TO DO MORE OF? WHAT ARE SOME NEW THINGS YOU WANT TO DO?

27. MY HAPPINESS IS MY DRIVE TOWARD FULFILLING MY GOALS. WHEN I BEGIN TO SEE THE VISION, I STRIVE TO BECOME ONE WITH THE WHOLE.

Quindell Evans

WHAT DO YOU DO FOR A LIVING? WHAT ARE YOUR 3 FAVORITE THINGS ABOUT IT?

28. MAY I CONDITION MYSELF WITH KINDNESS AND GRACE SO I CAN FOCUS ON THE GOAL EVEN WHEN THE OPPOSITION IS IN MY FACE.

WE LIKE TO SURROUND OURSELVES WITH PEOPLE OF LIKE MINDS BUT HOW CAN HAVING PEOPLE IN YOUR LIFE THAT THINK TOTALLY DIFFERENT FROM YOU HELP YOU?

29. I WANT TO LEARN TO LET GO AND FLOW WITH THE WIND. AT THE SAME TIME, I WANT TO ENSURE THAT I SEE MY VISION THROUGH TO THE END.

Quindell Evans

FEEL FREE TO EXPRESS YOURSELF AND REFLECT THROUGH WRITING, DRAWING OR ANY MEDIUM OF VISUALIZATION.

30. I GIVE THANKS TO YOU KNOWING THAT WE WILL BE EVERYTHING WE PLAN TO BE. THANKS FOR BEING MY FRIEND, MY COLLEAGUE, MY SUPPORTER & MY FAMILY.

WRITE A LETTER OF THANKS TO ANYONE OR TO MULTIPLE PEOPLE AT A TIME. YOU CAN KEEP IT FOR YOURSELF OR YOU CAN SHARE IT WITH THEM.

31. AS A LEADER, A HAPPY PLACE IS WHERE I MAKE MY WAY. SO THOSE WHO FOLLOW AND JOIN ME ARE GLAD TO STAY.

Quindell Evans

IF YOU COULD LIVE ANYWHERE IN THE WORLD, WHERE WOULD IT BE?

32. WHEN SOME THINGS DON'T GO MY WAY, I LET CHANGE FLOW. I USUALLY END UP LIKING THE WAY THINGS GO AND LEARN FROM THE GROWTH.

Quindell Evans

DESCRIBE A SITUATION WHERE THINGS DIDN'T GO THE WAY YOU PLANNED BUT YOU WERE SATISFIED WITH THE OUTCOME ANYWAY?

33. MAY I SPEAK LIFE, HAVE THE TASTE OF PROSPERITY AND EAT HEALTHY.

IF YOU COULD LIVE TO BE OVER 300 YEARS OLD, WOULD YOU WANT TO? WHY OR WHY NOT?

34. OF COURSE THERE ARE OBSTACLES ALONG THE WAY. I DON'T POINT THEM OUT TO DESTROY THEM. THAT WILL DRAIN ME. I FOCUS ON HOW TO AVOID THEM.

Quindell Evans

HOW CAN PROBLEMS PUSH YOU AND INSPIRE YOU INSTEAD OF HINDERING YOU?

35. I WORK ON WAYS TO WORK WITH EVERY OBSTACLE INSTEAD OF COMBATTING IT. THE KEY IS TO PLAN TO BE MORE PROACTIVE AND LESS REACTIVE.

DESCRIBE HOW AN ISSUE OR PROBLEM PUSHED YOU TO GROW INSTEAD OF HELD YOU BACK?

36. FROM THE BEGINNING I SEE MY VISION AND GOAL THROUGH TO THE END EVEN WHEN I DON'T KNOW HOW. I MOVE WITH MODERATION AND MANEUVER WITH BALANCE SO I CAN REMAIN ON MIDDLE GROUND.

Quindell Evans

DESCRIBE A SITUATION THAT CHANGED YOUR WHOLE OUTLOOK ON LIFE?

37. I PLAN TO PRODUCE A FARM THAT WILL PROVIDE FOOD FOR MY FAMILY EVERY NIGHT. UNTIL THEN, I PRACTICE BY WATERING THE PLANTS EVERYDAY AND PROVIDING THEM WITH LIGHT.

Quindell Evans

WHAT DO FOOD TO EAT, FOOD FOR THOUGHT AND FOOD FOR THE SOUL HAVE IN COMMON?

38. I REFLECT ON MYSELF. ALTHOUGH I MAY NOT LIKE SOME THINGS, I ACCEPT MY WHOLE SELF SO I MAY LIKE THE CHANGE.

Quindell Evans

DESCRIBE A HABIT YOU ONCE THOUGHT YOU COULDN'T LIVE WITHOUT DOING BUT NOW YOU ARE ABSOLUTELY FINE WITHOUT IT?

39. I FORGIVE MYSELF BUT I NEVER WANT TO FORGET MY PAST MISTAKES BECAUSE WHEN I LOOK BACK, I SEE MY GROWTH AND FEEL GREAT.

Quindell Evans

DESCRIBE AN OBJECT OR THING YOU ONCE THOUGHT YOU COULDN'T LIVE WITHOUT HAVING AND NOW YOU ARE ABSOLUTELY FINE WITHOUT IT?

40. I KNOW WHAT I WANT TO DO AND WHY. WHEN THE OPPORTUNITY IS A CHOICE, I AM PREPARED TO DECIDE.

Quindell Evans

WHAT IS YOUR BIGGEST DREAM(S)?

41. JUST AS THE EARTH GROWS AS SEASONS CHANGE THE WEATHER, MAY MY LIFE CONTINUE TO CHANGE FOR THE BETTER.

Quindell Evans

WHAT IS ONE ACCOMPLISHMENT YOU SAID YOU WERE GOING TO DO OR PLANNED AND NOW CAN SAY YOU DID IT?

42. I NURTURE AND PARTAKE IN MY PLANS WITH PATIENCE ON A DAILY BASIS. LIKE CHILDBIRTH, THE PROCESS OF PURSUING MY DREAMS IS LIKE HAVING A BABY.

Quindell Evans

WHAT ARE SOME INDICATORS THAT YOU ARE CLIMBING "YOUR" LADDER OF SUCCESS?

43. BEFORE BIRTH, I NURTURE MY IDEA IN THE WOMB OF MY MIND. AFTER BIRTH, I RAISE MY IDEA INTO REALITY, WITH NO RUSH, KNOWING THAT SUCCESS TAKES TIME.

Quindell Evans

WHAT ARE SOME THINGS THAT YOU DO THAT MAKES YOU FEEL YOUNG?

44. NO MORE WILL I ALLOW MY GOALS TO SLIP FROM UNDER ME. FROM NOW ON, AND NO MATTER HOW LONG, I WILL MAKE SURE TO SEE MY GOALS BECOMING ME.

WRITE DOWN 3 THINGS YOU COMMIT TO ACHIEVING OVER THE NEXT 12 MONTHS?

45. I KEEP A LIGHT HEART WHEN I CHANGE MY MIND. SO THAT I REMEMBER WHERE I STARTED AND REMAIN FOCUSED ON THE FINISH LINE/REMAIN FOCUSED ON THE PATH THAT'S MINE.

Quindell Evans

WHAT ARE SOME CHANGES YOU MADE OVER THE LAST YEAR?

46. THE SUNSET REMINDS ME THAT WHAT I WANT TO DO TOMORROW STARTS WITH TODAY'S PLANS. THE SUNRISE REMINDS ME THAT WHAT I WANTED TO DO YESTERDAY TODAY IS ANOTHER CHANCE.

Quindell Evans

WHAT ARE 3 THINGS YOU APPRECIATE ABOUT JUST BEING ALIVE?

47. TO SUCCEED, I PLAN TO MAKE PROACTIVE CHOICES OUT OF RATIONAL REFLECTION ON MY WORK ETHIC. I FOCUS ON WORKING WITH OTHERS WHO BRING OUT MY BEST AND RESPECT MY PROFESSION.

Quindell Evans

WHAT'S YOUR FAVORITE JOB YOU'VE EVER HAD OR COMPLETED?

48. MY DIET CONSISITS OF FOOD FOR THE SOUL AND FOOD FOR THOUGHT SO I CAN ALWAYS BE WILLING AND ABLE. I FOCUS ON COOKING WITH OTHERS WHO EAT TO HEAL SO I ACCEPT WHAT THEY BRING TO THE TABLE.

Quindell Evans

WHAT'S YOUR FAVORITE FOOD? IS IT HEALTHY OR NOT?

49. I DON'T RUN FROM A SITUATION THAT I FEEL I CANT HANDLE. I LEARN TO RUN THE SITUATION AND HANDLE IT WITH CONCRETE PLANNING.

IF YOU ARE RIGHT HANDED, WRITE YOUR NAME AND SIGNATURE WITH YOUR LEFT HAND. IF YOU ARE LEFT HANED, WRITE YOUR NAME AND SIGNATURE WITH YOUR RIGHT HAND.

50. I LOVE WHAT I GOT PLANNED SO IM HAPPY DOING THE WORK THAT I DO. I FEEL LIKE I GROW, EXPAND AND IMPROVE WHEN I DO SOMETHING DIFFICULT OR NEW. (SO BRING IT ON.)

Quindell Evans

WHERE IS ONE NEW PLACE YOU WANT TO GO OR HAVE BEEN THIS WEEK? WHAT DID YOU LEARN?

51. I ENJOY LISTENING TO OTHERS EVEN WHEN THEY'RE EXPLAINING THINGS I DON'T AGREE WITH. SO I CAN LEARN HOW THEY FUNCTION AND GET TO KNOW WHAT THEY BELIEVE IN.

: ?
DESCRIBE HOW THE WORLD WOULD BE IF EVERYONE LOOKED, THOUGHT AND ACTED THE SAME? WOULD IT BE BETTER OR WORSE? DO WE NEED DIFFERENCES?

52. THE MORE I CONTINUE TO PRACTICE MAKING DESCIONS OUT OF SELF-LOVE AND CREATIVITY, I REALIZE I'M THE MASTER OF MY OWN DESTINY NO MATTER WHAT ANYONE ELSE HAS DONE TO ME, FOR ME OR GIVEN ME.

HOW CAN YOU USE YOUR PAST TRAUMA OR MISTAKES TO HELP YOURSELF OR SOMEONE ELSE TODAY?

53. ALONG THIS JOURNEY OF LIVING MY DREAMS, I MAY MAKE A WRONG DECISION THAT MOMENTARILY FEELS RIGHT. THAT ALLOWS ME TO LEARN ABOUT MYSELF AND HOW I GROW THROUGH LIFE, NOT GO THROUGH LIFE.

Quindell Evans

WHAT'S THE DIFFERENCE BETWEEN GOING THROUGH AND GROWING THROUGH?

54. PATIENCE INSTEAD OF WAITING, COMPASSION INSTEAD OF PASSIVE, INSTEAD OF AGGRESSION, ACCEPTANCE OF OTHERS' AND MINE IMPERFECTIONS.

Quindell Evans

WHAT'S THE DIFFERENCE BETWEEN WAITING AND BEING PATIENT?

55. FRUSTRATION IS PRESSURE AND A POWER THAT PUTS DOWN MORE THAN LIFTING ANYONE HIGHER. BUT, GENTLE KINDNESS WILL TAME AND LEAD THE WILDEST LION.

Quindell Evans

WHY IS IT IMPORTANT TO BE KIND EVEN WHEN SOMEONE ISN'T? WHY NOT BE MEAN BACK TO THEM?

56. I DON'T FOCUS ON WHAT I DON'T KNOW WHEN I'M PURSUING SOMETHING NEW. I FOCUS ON USING THE TOOLS THAT I ALREADY HAVE TO MY FULL POTENTIAL.

WHAT IS ONE GOAL YOU HAVE? WHAT KNOWLEDGE DO YOU HAVE OF HOW TO COMPLETE IT? WHAT DO YOU WANT/NEED TO KNOW IN ORDER TO COMPLETE IT? WHAT HAVE YOU LEARNED BY JUST TRYING?

57. THE KEY TO DOING THE IMPOSSIBLE: KEEP DOING WHAT'S POSSIBLE.

Quindell Evans

SPELL "I'M" AND THEN SAY "POSSIBLE."

58. WORDS ARE POWER BUT YOU DON'T SIMPLY BECOME EVERYTHING THAT YOU SAID. ACTIONS SPEAK LOUDER THAN WORDS SO GET THINGS DONE BY THINKING AHEAD.

Quindell Evans

WRITE A LETTER TO YOUR FUTURE SELF, (10 YEARS FROM NOW) THANKING YOURSELF FOR WHAT YOU ENVISION ACHIEVING.

59. WORDS ARE POWER, SO I CAN SPEAK LIMITATIONS, CIRCUMSTANCES AND OBSTACLES AGAINST ME. BUT I CHOOSE TO DO RIGHT AND USE MY WORDS TO UPLIFT ME.

WRITE DOWN SOME GOALS ON A SEPARATE PAPER AND RECITE THEM ALOUD THEN BURN THE PAPER.

60. PURSUING MY GOALS REQUIRES ME TO BE AMBITIOUS ALONG THE BUMPY RIDE. THROUGH CONSISTENT SELF REFLECTION, I TRUST MY DREAMS AND INTUITION TO BE MY GUIDE.

WRITE DOWN ANY DREAMS YOU REMEMBER. IF YOU NEED HELP REMEMBERING YOUR DREAMS DROP A FEW DROPLETS OF TEA TREE, LAVENDER OR EUCALYPTUS ESSENTIAL OIL ON YOUR PILLOW.

61. SOMETIMES, IN ORDER TO CHANGE & START DOING SOMETHING NEW, AN OLD HABIT HAS TO BE CUT OUT. OTHER TIMES, STOPPING AN OLD HABIT REQUIRES FINDING A NEW ROUTE.

WHAT ARE SOME HABITS YOU WANT TO CUT OUT OF YOUR LIFE OR SLOW DOWN ON? WHAT CAN YOU DO TO REPLACE THEM?

**62. I'VE BEEN WATERING THE SEEDS OF MY DREAMS FOR SOME TIME NOW AND I'VE SEEN MY FIRST BUD GROW TODAY.
WITH PATIENCE AND PLANS, I'LL CONTINUE TO PROVIDE MY DREAMS THE WORK IT NEEDS UNTIL I CAN CREATE A WHOLE BOUQUET.**

WHAT DO YOU DO FOR WORK? WHAT MAKES YOU HAPPY ABOUT IT? WHAT KEEPS YOU GOING?

**63. I DON'T BELIEVE IN OPPOSITES.
I BELIEVE IN COMPLIMENTS BECAUSE
OPPOSITES ATTRACT. THEY DON'T COMBAT.**

Quindell Evans

WHAT'S THE OPPOSITE OF FEAR?
WHAT'S THE OPPOSITE OF TRUST?
WHAT'S THE OPPOSITE OF LOVE?
WHAT'S THE OPPOSITE OF MALE?
DO WE NEED OPPOSITES? WHY?

64. TWO PEOPLE OF UNLIKE MINDS CAN WORK TOGETHER SUCCESSFULLY TOWARD ONE CAUSE. OPPOSITES ATTRACT, NOT COMBAT. IT'S UNIVERSAL LAW.

Quindell Evans

WHAT ARE SOME THINGS YOU ONCE BELIEVED OR FELT VERY STRONG ABOUT AND NOW YOU DON'T AGREE WITH OR FEEL THE TOTAL OPPOSITE?

65. RESPONSIBILITY IS THE ABILITY TO RESPOND TO THE VISION OF MY DREAMS & GOALS. I AM RESPONSIBLE BY TAKING ACTION, ORGANIZING, PREPARING AND PRACTICING SELF CONTROL.

WHAT ARE SOME THINGS THAT TRIGGER YOU? SOME THINGS THAT YOU SEE OR EXPERIENCE THAT MAKES YOU SMILE AND LAUGH. SOME THINGS THAT YOU SEE OR EXPERIENCE THAT BRINGS OUT YOUR ANGER OR SADNESS.

66. THERE'S ALWAYS NEW THINGS I WANT TO DO OR THINGS I WANT TO DO MORE OF & WANT TO DO LESS. BUT I SEE GROWTH IN EVERY PART OF ME, EVEN THE ONES I FEEL AREN'T THE BEST.

CAN YOU CONTROL YOUR ANGER, FRUSTRATION AND SADNESS WHEN IT IS TRIGGERED? DO YOU FEEL THESE EMOTIONS ARE NEEDED SOMETIMES OR DO YOU WANT TO STOP FEELING THESE FOREVER?

67. I WORK ON WAYS TO PERSONALLY BETTER MYSELF AND IMPROVE SO I CAN BRING THE BEST ME TO OTHERS IN ANY ROOM.

DO YOU FEEL LIKE THERE ARE PEOPLE WHO CAN JUST BRING THE WORST OUT OF YOU? WHAT DO YOU THINK YOU CAN DO TO BE MORE PREPARED AND IN CONTROL OF YOURSELF?

68. FORM FOLLOWS FUNCTION. I GET WHAT I WANT BY USING WHAT I HAVE ALREADY. IN A GROUP SETTING, WE EACH IDENTIFY OUR ROLES TO MAKE SURE WE ARE ALL READY.

DO YOU FEEL LIKE THERE ARE PEOPLE WHO JUST BRING OUT THE BEST IN YOU AND INSPIRE YOU? WHO ARE THOSE PEOPLE AND WHAT IS YOUR RELATIONSHIP LIKE WITH THEM? WHY DO YOU SUPPOSE THEY INSPIRE YOU?

69. ORGANIZATION IS ARRANGING WHAT YOU HAVE INTO THE STRUCTURE OF WHAT YOU WANT BY PLANNING HOW TO GET THERE...WITH CONFIDENCE NOT FEAR.

Quindell Evans

DO YOU FEEL LIKE WHAT YOU DREAM OR ASPIRE TO BE IS TOO LARGE FOR YOU? DOES IT SCARE YOU TO START PURSUING YOUR DREAMS? WHY OR WHY NOT?

70. OTHER PEOPLE'S OPINION OF ME DOES NOT HAVE TO BECOME MY REALITY. BECAUSE I MAKE THE CHOICES AND DECISIONS TO DO WHAT I WANT AND LIVE HAPPILY.

WHAT ARE SOME NEGATIVE COMMENTS THAT SOMEONE HAS TOLD YOU ABOUT YOURSELF THAT HAS STUCK IN YOUR HEAD? WHAT ARE SOME POSITIVE COMMENTS OR ADVICE SOMEONE GAVE YOU THAT YOU WILL ALWAYS REMEMBER?

71. I REALIZE THAT OPPORTUNITIES ARE EVER PRESENT. FUTURE SUCCESS BEGINS WITH PREPARATION IN THE PRESENCE.

Quindell Evans

WHAT'S THE DIFFERENCE BETWEEN THE PAST, THE PRESENT AND THE FUTURE? WHICH ONE MATTERS MOST TO YOU?

72. AS I WORK TOWARD COMPLETING MY GOALS, I CAN SEE AND FEEL MY TRANSFORMATION. I AM GETTING TO KNOW MYSELF MORE BY FINDING MY BALANCE & CREATING ORGANIZATION.

Quindell Evans

WHAT ARE SOME TALENTS YOU'VE DISCOVERED IN YOURSELF OR HABITS THAT YOU'VE GROWN TO ENJOY THAT YOU NEVER KNEW YOU WOULD?

73. WHAT I IMAGINE IN MY MIND, I USE IT TO CREATE IN MY WORK. I BALANCE MY EMOTIONS WITH THE TIMES SO I CAN CREATE CLEARLY WHEN I'M HAPPY OR HURT.

DESCRIBE A SITUATION WHERE YOUR EMOTIONS DISTRACTED YOU OR GOT THE BEST OF YOU? WRITE DOWN THE GOALS THAT YOU COULD HAVE FOCUSED ON TO REDIRECT YOU.

74. MY DAILY HABITS AND BEHAVIORS HELPS DEVELOP MY CHARACTER AND PERSONALITY THAT I LIVE IN THE FUTURE WITH. SO WITH MY GOOD HABITS, I USE IT BEFORE I LOSE IT. AND WITH MY NEGATIVE BEHAVIORS, I LOSE IT BEFORE I GET USED TO IT.

Quindell Evans

WHAT ARE SOME THINGS YOU WANT TO BE ABLE TO DO FOREVER? WHAT ARE SOME THINGS YOU WANT TO WORK ON OR STOP BEFORE IT BEGINS TO SLOW YOU DOWN OR HURT YOU?

75. BODILY HEALTH IS PHYSICAL EXERCISE, AND WHAT I CHOOSE TO EAT TODAY. MENTAL HEALTH, IS WILLINGNESS TO LEARN, AND WHAT I CHOOSE TO SPEAK TODAY. EMOTIONAL/SPIRITUAL HEALTH IS GIVING THANKS FOR THE MOMENT, AND WHAT I CHOOSE TO BE TODAY.

WHAT CAN YOU DO TO CONTINUE BALANCING YOUR PHSYICAL HEALTH? WHAT CAN YO DO TO CONTINUE ENHANCING YOUR MENTAL HEALTH? WHAT CAN YOU DO TO CONTINUE CONTROLLING YOUR EMOTIONS AND SPIRITUAL HEALTH?

76. I REFLECT WITH PATIENCE AND PLAN TO FUNCTION WITH THE RIGHT FLOW SO I AM PREPARED TO PURSUE MY DAYDREAMS & NIGHT GOALS.

Quindell Evans

WHAT ARE SOME THINGS YOU OFTEN DAYDREAM ABOUT? DO YOU FEEL THESE ARE DISTRACTIONS AND OVERTHINKING OR DO YOUR DAYDREAMS ENHANCE YOUR IDEAS?

77. I WANT TO CHANGE SOME THINGS IN MY LIFE & I KNOW CHANGE BEGINS WITHIN MYSELF. I ADD NEW THINGS IN MY DAILY ROUTINES SO I CAN START SEEING NEW RESULTS.

Quindell Evans

WHAT IS ONE NEW THING YOU CAN DO THAT YOU ALWAYS WANTED TO TRY? IS THERE A PLACE YOU'VE NEVER BEEN THAT YOU FEEL WILL HELP IF YOU WENT?

78. I APPRECIATE ALL MY SETBACKS AND DISTRACTIONS FOR HELPING ME WAKE UP. I APPRECIATE ALL MY ADVANCEMENTS AND ENHANCEMENTS FOR HELPING ME STAY UP.

Quindell Evans

WHAT ARE SOME PAINFUL OR TRAUMATIC EXPERIENCES THAT YOU FEEL ACTUALLY MADE YOU A BETTER PERSON INSTEAD OF HINDERING YOU? HOW?

79. IT MAKES ME HAPPY TO PLAN & SET CLEAR GOALS. WHEN I COMPLETE MY GOALS, IT MAKES ME FEEL WHOLE.

Quindell Evans

WHAT IS A BUSINESS THAT YOU'VE ALWAYS SEEN YOURSELF RUNNING? ARE YOU A BUSINESS OWNER NOW? WHY DO YOU FEEL THIS BUSINESS SUITS YOU?

80. I WORK ON CONTROLLING MYSELF SO WHEN THINGS ARE OUT OF MY CONTROL, I CAN ALWAYS FOCUS ON MY GOALS.

Quindell Evans

FEEL FREE TO EXPRESS YOURSELF AND REFLECT THROUGH WRITING, DRAWING OR ANY MEDIUM OF VISUALIZATION.

81. I DON'T RESIST CHANGE AND GO AGAINST THE FLOW. I GO WITH THE CHANGE AS AN OPPORTUNITY TO GROW.

Quindell Evans

DESCRIBE A CIRCUMSTANCE THAT YOU DIDN'T EXPECT TO EXPERIENCE THAT CHANGED YOU FOR THE BETTER.

82. I LIKE PLANNING AND EMBARKING ON NEW VENTURES. I AM LETTING GO OF OLD HABITS TO FOCUS ON NEW TRADITIONS.

WHAT IS ONE THING YOU FEEL YOU CAN'T GO ONE DAY WITHOUT? DON'T DO THAT FOR ONE DAY.

83. I VALUE WHAT I HAVE WAY MORE THAN I WANT BECAUSE I UTILIZE WHAT I HAVE IN ORDER TO GET WHAT I WANT DONE.

Quindell Evans

DO YOU FEEL YOU HAVE EVERYTHING YOU NEED TO SUCCEED? IF NOT, WHAT DO YOU FEEL YOU NEED TO POSSESS OR LEARN?

84. I'M CONTINUALLY BUILDING MY CHARACTER TO BE MORE BALANCED AND LESS BIAS SO THAT I CAN ALLOW THE PURPOSE OF POLARITIES TO PUSH ME TO FUNCTION AT MY HIGHEST.

Quindell Evans

WHAT IS POLARITY? IS IT A GOOD THING OR A BAD THING? HOW DOES IT APPLY TO YOU?

85. THE POPULAR THING TO DO IS NOT ALWAYS RIGHT. THE RIGHT THING TO DO IS NOT ALWAYS KIND. I STRIVE TO ALWAYS DO THE RIGHT THING AND BE KIND TO KEEP A PEACE OF MIND.

Quindell Evans

WHAT ARE SOME THINGS THAT YOU FEEL ARE COMMON AND TRENDY IN THE WORLD THAT ISN'T RIGHT OR THE BEST THING TO DO?

86. MY COURAGE TO SUCCEED OUTWEIGHS MY FEAR OF NOT SUCCEEDING. TO WAKE UP AND BREATHE IS ALL THE REASON TO KEEP DREAMING.

Quindell Evans

WHY DO WE AS PEOPLE SET BIG GOALS FOR OURSELVES INSTEAD OF JUST LIVING MINIMALLY OR ESSENTIALLY WITH WHATEVER IS PROVIDED NATURALLY?

87. DOING THE SAME THINGS MAKES ME FEEL OLD & DOING NEW THINGS MAKES ME FEEL YOUNG. TO SUSTAIN MY GROWTH, I DO BOTH BECAUSE EITHER WAY CHANGE IS GOING TO COME.

Quindell Evans

WHAT ARE SOME THINGS THAT REMINDS YOU THAT YOU'RE AGING AND WHAT ARE SOME ACTIVITIES THAT MAKE YOU FEEL YOUNG?

88. I KEEP MY EXPECTATIONS HIGH AND MY ASSUMPTIONS LOW SO I AM ABLE TO CHANGE WITH THE TIMES AND LET STAGNATION GO.

Quindell Evans

HOW DO YOU FEEL WHEN PEOPLE ACKNOWLEDGE THAT YOU ARE CHANGING? DOES BEING ACCEPTED MATTER TO YOU? WHY?

89. I AM A LEADER WHO INNERSTAND THAT LEADING IS MORE ABOUT LEARNING THAN TEACHING. THE MORE I LEARN ABOUT MYSELF THE BETTER I AM AT WORKING WITH OTHER PEOPLE.

WHEN YOU WERE IN SCHOOL, DO YOU FEEL LIKE YOU LEARNED MORE OR BETTER FROM TEACHERS YOU RELATED TO OR TEACHERS THAT WERE DIFFERENT FROM YOU? WHY AND HOW?

90. I FEEL THAT EVERYTHING IS ALL RIGHT AND I VALUE SELF-HEALING AS THE HEAD OF MY PLAN. I APPRECIATE THE PEOPLE IN MY LIFE AND TRUST THAT WHEN NEEDED THEY WILL LEND A HELPING HAND.

Quindell Evans

ARE YOU MORE COMFORTABLE WORKING ALONE OR DO YOU OFTEN ASK FOR HELP WHEN YOU FEEL YOU NEED IT? WHY?

91. TAKING ADVANTAGE OF THE OPPPORTUNITY TO PURSUE MY DREAMS SOMETIMES MEANS TRADING IN WHAT I'M MOST COMFORTBALE DOING FOR BRAND NEW THINGS.

WHAT ARE SOME NEW THINGS YOU CAN ADD TO YOUR DAILY HABITS THAT MAY HELP YOU BETTER FOCUS ON YOUR SUCCESS? WHAT ARE SOME THINGS YOU ARE CURRENTLY DOING THAT YOU FEEL YOU SHOULD CONTINUE?

92. I AM PURSUING MY DREAMS, NOT ILLUSIONS. I FOCUS ON BUILDING ON CLEAR VISIONS AND NOT GETTING CAUGHT IN CONFUSION.

Quindell Evans

HOW MAY YOU OR HOW ARE YOU HELPING OTHERS WHILE PURSUING YOUR DREAMS?

93. I ACCEPT, APPRECIATE AND AM MORE WILLING TO SUPPORT OTHER PEOPLE'S GOALS BY BALANCING MY EMOTIONS AND FOCUSING ON HAVING SELF CONTROL.

Quindell Evans

IN WHAT WAYS CAN HELPING SOMEONE ELSE COMPLETE HIS OR HER GOALS BE BENIFICIAL FOR YOUR OWN SUCCESS?

94. THE MORE CONSISTENT I AM TO SUCCEED, THE MORE CONFIDENT I BECOME AND THE MORE CLEARLY I CAN ENVISION MY DREAMS. INSTEAD OF FRONTING LIKE I'M FEARLESS, I CONFRONT THE FEARS PLANTED IN ME AND CHOOSE TO NOT WATER THEIR SEEDS.

Quindell Evans

WHAT ARE THE SCARIEST PARTS OF PURSUING YOUR DREAMS? WHAT ARE SOME THINGS THAT MAKE YOU FEEL LIKE YOU CAN FAIL? WRITE DOWN WAYS TO OVERCOME THESE FEARS AND HOW YOU WILL BE ABLE TO KEEP GOING AFTER FAILING.

95. I CHOSE TO START CREATING MY TRANSFORMATION INSTEAD OF WAITING FOR SOMETHING TO FORCE ME TO CHANGE. I NOTICED THAT BY INITIATING MY OWN GROWTH, I APPRECIATED THE SUPPORT THAT CAME.

Quindell Evans

HOW DO THE PEOPLE IN YOUR LIFE ASSIST AND SUPPORT YOUR DREAMS AND GOALS? IF THEY STOPPED, DO YOU FEEL STRONG AND GROUNDED ENOUGH TO CONTINUE?

96. THE MORE I WORK ON MY GROWTH, THE MORE CLEARER & VIVID MY DREAMS ARE. WITH MORE CONFIDENCE & CLARITY, I AM ABLE TO FOCUS ON SUCCEEDING EVEN WHEN IT SEEMS HARD.

DESCRIBE A SITUATION WHERE WORKING ON YOUR GOALS AND DREAMS HELPED YOU GET YOUR MIND OFF A TRAUMATIC OR CONTROVERSIAL EXPERIENCE.

97. I MAKE DECISIONS TO DELIBERATELY ACHIEVE MY GOALS. THAT MEANS I TAKE THE NECESSARY TIME TO PLAN SO THAT MY VISION IS WHOLE.

CREATE A 5-YEAR TIMELINE OF THINGS YOU WANT TO ACHIEVE IN THE ORDER YOU ENVISION.

98. I FORGIVE MYSELF FOR MISTAKES SO I CAN FOCUS ON WHAT'S GREAT INSTEAD OF ALLOWING REGRET TO BLIND ME WITH SELF-HATE.

WHAT ARE SOME MISTAKES YOU'VE MADE THAT CAUSED YOU TO HURT YOURSELF OR SOMEONE ELSE. WRITE THEM DOWN AND SAY OUT LOUD "I FORGIVE MYSELF" FOR EACH OF THEM.

99. PURPOSE IS THE PIECE TO MY PUZZLE THAT TRANSFORMS IT INTO A MAP WHERE NO MATTER WHICH PATH I TAKE I'M ALWAYS ON THE RIGHT TRACK.

… Quindell Evans

WHAT DO YOU FEEL LIKE IS THE OVERALL MEANING OF LIFE?

100. I AM HAPPY WITH EVERYTHING THAT I HAVE AND BELIEVE IN MY ABILITY TO SUCCEEED. WHETHER OR NOT I HAVE EVERYTHING THAT I WANT, I KNOW THAT I HAVE EVERYTHING THAT I NEED.

# WRITE DOWN ALL THE REASONS WHY YOU FEEL YOU'RE A GOOD PERSON.

ABOUT THE AUTHOR

Quindell Evans is a music recording artist from New York City having recorded and released a handful of musical projects such as *Give Them Moor*, *The Moor They Want* and *Moor Than Black* on all digital musical stores. Quindell extends his talents as a teaching artist in NYC using his life experiences to guide those in need of healing through poetry and creative writing workshops.

Visit him at BluePoetTree.com